Adam falls to Earth

Written by: Abbass Noureddin
Illustrated by: Tahera Amini
Translated by: Amal Abdallah

Copyright © 2021 by Lantern Publications

All rights reserved. No part of this publication may be reproduced, distributed, or transmitted in any form or by any means, including photocopying, recording, or other electronic or mechanical methods, without the prior written permission of the publisher, except in the case of brief quotations embodied in critical reviews and certain other noncommercial uses permitted by copyright law. For permission requests, write to the publisher, addressed "Attention: - Permissions (Adam Falls to Earth)," at the email address below.

Lantern Publications
info@lanternpublications.com
www.lanternkids.com.au

Ordering Information:
Quantity sales. Special discounts are available on quantity purchases by corporations,
associations, and others. For details, contact the distributor at the address above.

ISBN- 978-1-922583-14-7

First Edition

Adam Falls to Earth

Abbass Noureddin

﴿وَلَقَدْ خَلَقْنَا الْإِنْسَانَ مِنْ سُلَالَةٍ مِنْ طِينٍ﴾ المؤمنون ـ الآية 12

﴿وَخَلَقَ الْجَانَّ مِنْ مَارِجٍ مِنْ نَارٍ﴾ الرحمن ـ الآية 15

{We created man from an extract of clay} The Believers 23:12
{And created the jinn from a flame of a fire} The Compassionate 55:15

God created fire, water, mud, and light.
He created the angels from light.
He created the jinn from a smokeless fire.
And He created man from water and mud.

God wanted His greatness to be seen in His greatest creature.
But who is God's greatest creature?!
Is it the angels, the jinn, or is it man?
It was the Earth that held the answer to this question.

God created the Earth to be a racetrack for the angels,
the jinn and man.
Whoever reforms Earth, will be God's greatest creature,
because God's ability will be revealed through him.

﴿وَإِذْ قَالَ رَبُّكَ لِلْمَلَائِكَةِ إِنِّي جَاعِلٌ فِي الْأَرْضِ خَلِيفَةً قَالُوا أَتَجْعَلُ فِيهَا مَنْ يُفْسِدُ فِيهَا وَيَسْفِكُ الدِّمَاءَ وَنَحْنُ نُسَبِّحُ بِحَمْدِكَ وَنُقَدِّسُ لَكَ قَالَ إِنِّي أَعْلَمُ مَا لَا تَعْلَمُونَ﴾

سورة البقرة - الآية 30

{ When your Sustainer said unto the angels: "Behold, I am about to establish upon earth one who shall inherit it." They said, "Will You place in it someone who will cause corruption in it and shed blood, while we declare Your praises and sanctify You?" He said, "I know what you do not know."} The Cow 1:30

The angels were fast at obeying, so they thought that they will win the test.

The jinn, who were swift, fiery and highly energetic, also thought that they will win the race.

As for man, he was somewhere between dust and water.

But then God declared the winner:

It was Man!

Man will be God's representative on Earth!

The Angels were astonished, for they had always been working obediently for God.

Iblis, the head of the jinn, was furious because he worshipped God for six thousand years!

When the angels asked God about His choice, He asked them about the reality of things, but they did not know the answer.

God also ordered Iblis to wait until he knows why God favored Adam over him.

Then, it was man's turn to be tested.

Will he be ready to reform Earth?

﴿وَعَلَّمَ آدَمَ الْأَسْمَاءَ كُلَّهَا ثُمَّ عَرَضَهُمْ عَلَى الْمَلَائِكَةِ فَقَالَ أَنْبِئُونِي بِأَسْمَاءِ هَٰؤُلَاءِ إِنْ كُنْتُمْ صَادِقِينَ * قَالُوا سُبْحَانَكَ لَا عِلْمَ لَنَا إِلَّا مَا عَلَّمْتَنَا إِنَّكَ أَنْتَ الْعَلِيمُ الْحَكِيمُ﴾

البقرة ـ الآية 31

{And He taught Adam the names, all of them; then he presented them to the angels, and said, "Tell Me the names of these, if you are sincere." They said, "Glory be to You! We have no knowledge except what You have taught us. It is You who are the Knowledgeable, the Wise."} The Cow 1:31,32

God taught Adam the names. Each and every name speaks of the reality of things. Meanwhile the angels were busy glorifying God and reforming things.

Then God asked the angels about these names.

The angels did not know the answer, so they realised that they cannot reform the Earth.

﴿قَالَ يَا آدَمُ أَنبِئْهُم بِأَسْمَائِهِمْ فَلَمَّا أَنبَأَهُم بِأَسْمَائِهِمْ قَالَ أَلَمْ أَقُل لَّكُمْ إِنِّي أَعْلَمُ غَيْبَ السَّمَاوَاتِ وَالْأَرْضِ وَأَعْلَمُ مَا تُبْدُونَ وَمَا كُنتُمْ تَكْتُمُونَ﴾

البقرة ـ الآية 33

{He said, "O Adam, inform them of their names." And when he had informed them of their names, He said, "Did I not tell you that I know the secrets of the heavens and the earth, and that I know what you reveal and what you conceal?"} The Cow 1:33

Then God brought Adam in front of the angels, and ordered him to explain all the realities to them. So, Adam started teaching the angels.

Now the angels were no longer astonished and realised God's wisdom in choosing Adam. And because the angels loved and obeyed God, they rejoiced over the new vicegerent, and decided to help him.

﴿وَإِذْ قُلْنَا لِلْمَلَائِكَةِ اسْجُدُوا لِآدَمَ فَسَجَدُوا إِلَّا إِبْلِيسَ أَبَىٰ وَاسْتَكْبَرَ وَكَانَ مِنَ الْكَافِرِينَ﴾ البقرة ـ الآية 34

﴿قَالَ مَا مَنَعَكَ أَلَّا تَسْجُدَ إِذْ أَمَرْتُكَ قَالَ أَنَا خَيْرٌ مِنْهُ خَلَقْتَنِي مِنْ نَارٍ وَخَلَقْتَهُ مِنْ طِينٍ﴾ الأعراف ـ الآية 12

{And We said to the angels, "Prostrate to Adam." They prostrated, except for Iblis. He refused, and acted arrogantly, and was one of the faithless} Heifer 34

{ He [God] said "What prevented you from prostrating when I commanded you?" "I am better than Him' He [Iblis] said; "You created me from fire, and You created him from mud"}
The Elevations 7:12

Then it was the turn of Iblis, but he acted proudly.

Iblis refused to prostrate and said, "I am better than Adam, and more capable of reforming Earth."

So God placed Adam in a lofty garden and allowed Satan to view and observe him.

Adam preserved that garden, he neither corrupted nor polluted it.

﴿ وَقُلْنَا يَا آدَمُ اسْكُنْ أَنتَ وَزَوْجُكَ الْجَنَّةَ وَكُلَا مِنْهَا رَغَدًا حَيْثُ شِئْتُمَا وَلَا تَقْرَبَا هَذِهِ الشَّجَرَةَ فَتَكُونَا مِنَ الظَّالِمِينَ ﴾

البقرة ـ الآية 35

{We said, "O Adam, stay with your spouse in the garden, and eat from it freely as you please, but do not approach this tree, lest you should be among the wrongdoers."} Cow 1:35

Satan's heart burned with hatred.

He decided to prove to God that Adam cannot preserve this garden. Satan had a plan!

There was a tree in this garden, which God had warned Adam and Eve about.

God said, "Do not approach it now, because if you do, you will not be able to stay in the lofty garden."

Satan decided to convince Adam and Eve to taste from the tree, so they fail the test.

﴿ فَأَزَلَّهُمَا الشَّيْطَانُ عَنْهَا فَأَخْرَجَهُمَا مِمَّا كَانَا فِيهِ وَقُلْنَا اهْبِطُوا بَعْضُكُمْ لِبَعْضٍ عَدُوٌّ وَلَكُمْ فِي الْأَرْضِ مُسْتَقَرٌّ وَمَتَاعٌ إِلَىٰ حِينٍ ﴾

البقرة ـ الآية 36

{But Satan caused them to stumble from it, and dislodged them from the state they were in. We [God] said, "Go down, some of you enemies of one another. And you will have residence on earth, and enjoyment for a while."} Cow 1:36

Satan came to Adam and Eve and said, "God ordered you not to approach that tree, so that you do not become immortal and live forever."

Adam was unaware of Satan's enmity. He thought that Satan was advising him for his own good and forgot what God had told him about the tree!

Satan continued to whisper to Adam and Eve, until he convinced them to taste of the tree!

﴿قُلْنَا اهْبِطُوا مِنْهَا جَمِيعًا فَإِمَّا يَأْتِيَنَّكُمْ مِنِّي هُدًى فَمَنْ تَبِعَ هُدَايَ فَلَا خَوْفٌ عَلَيْهِمْ وَلَا هُمْ يَحْزَنُونَ﴾

البقرة - الآية 38

{We said, "Go down from it, all of you. Yet whenever guidance comes to you from Me, then whoever follows My guidance—they have nothing to fear, nor shall they grieve.} Cow 1:38

Satan was delighted when Adam obeyed him. He knew that God will banish Adam from the lofty garden before he accomplishes his mission. But then, there was the great surprise!

After Adam tasted the tree, God placed him and his wife on Earth. So, Satan thought that now he can control Adam and his children and offspring, and prevent them from being God's vicegerents on Earth. But God the Almighty brought great tidings to Adam!

God told Adam that the day will come when one of his offspring will reform Earth and fulfill the mission.

﴿فَتَلَقَّىٰ آدَمُ مِنْ رَبِّهِ كَلِمَاتٍ فَتَابَ عَلَيْهِ إِنَّهُ هُوَ التَّوَّابُ الرَّحِيمُ﴾

البقرة ـ الآية 37

{ Thereupon Adam received words [of guidance] from his Sustainer, and He accepted his repentance: for, verily, He alone is the Acceptor of Repentance, the Dispenser of Grace.} Cow 1:37

Adam and the angels rejoiced over this news.

Now, Adam regretted tasting that tree, and asked God for repentance and forgiveness.

The answer for Adam's request came.

"Because you rejoiced over the savior, I will accept your repentance. And when the savior arises, you shall return with him to a loftier garden".

﴿ قَالَ فَبِعِزَّتِكَ لَأُغْوِيَنَّهُمْ أَجْمَعِينَ ﴾   ص _ الآية 82

{He said, "By Your majesty, I will seduce them all."} Saad 38:82

The angels understood man's great secret. They understood that if man loves God's allies and repents for his sins, he will be able to reform Earth.

As for Satan, his grudge and loathing for man grew stronger. He decided to do his best so that Adam's offspring become enemies to the savior of mankind, and never seek forgiveness!

So, what happened next?

You will know in the coming stories.

MORE READING

Arastu .R., *Gods Emissaries – From Adam to Jesus* (2019), Imam Mahdi Association of Marjaeya (IMAM)- A brilliant book to get more details on the life of Prophet Adam (as)

Khomaini R.M, *Forty Hadith* (1939) Translated by Ali Quli Qarai and Maliha Qarai (1996) Ansariyan Publications. (4th Hadith on Kibr) (also available on al-islam.org)

www.ingramcontent.com/pod-product-compliance
Lightning Source LLC
Chambersburg PA
CBHW051251110526
44588CB00025B/2954